THIS IS GOING TO HURT

THE TRUTH
ALWAYS DOES

MICHAEL ERNEST

MICHAEL ERNEST

Printed in the United States of America
First Printing 2022
First Edition 2022

ISBN: 978-1-7372773-0-9 (Paperback Edition)

ISBN: 978-1-7372773-1-6 (e-Book Edition)

Library of Congress Control Number: 2021916257

10 9 8 7 6 5 4 3 2 1

For more information, contact:
Email: Turnedgorilla@gmail.com
Website: https://www.youtube.com/channel/UCGax-Q0zd32QNJv076G58Yw
Imperial x Rottweilers LLC

THIS IS GOING TO HURT
THE TRUTH ALWAYS DOES

TWERK THE OPPS

FUCK BOY

YAAASS

BEEF

BABY MOTHER

BYE FELICIA SQUAD

NO CAP

SHADE FLEE

NI**AZ PLUGS

RACHET

BAE

BABY DADDY

Table of Contents

About The Author....................1
Dedication....................3
Acknowledgments....................5
Preface....................7
Disclaimer....................9
Little Ni**az Turned Gorilla....................11
Introduction....................13
Chapter 1....................23
Economic Sovereignty
Chapter 2....................38
Child Support Hurts The So-Called
"Black Community"
More Than It Helps It!
Chapter 3....................49
Black Mothers vs. Breastfeeding
Chapter 4....................60
The Wrap-Up – Breaking The Chains of Servitude
Get Conscious. Your People Depend On It!
Little Ni**az Turned Gorilla....................71
Appendix....................73
Authors Notes....................77
Selected Bibliography....................79
Upcoming Publications....................85

About The Author

Brother Michael Ernest is a graduate of Lincoln University, formerly known as Ashmun Institute, the first degree-granting Historically Black College and University (HBCU) in the United States, where he earned a B.S. Degree in Criminal Justice. Brother Michael continued his educational pursuits and acquired a Master's Degree from Wilmington University, College of Social and Behavioral Sciences.

His contributions to join several organizations to promote human welfare include being a proud brother of Iota Phi Theta Fraternity Incorporated and Member of the National Association for the Advancement of Colored People (NAACP) to continue the fight irrespective of race, religion, or political affiliation. His numerous and beneficial efforts include, but are not limited to, historian contributions to social, intellectual, and advancements of Black Greek Letter Organization on Historically Black Colleges and Universities.

Brother Michael has focused study for many weeks, months, and years to compile an arsenal of knowledge and resources (writings, websites, book referrals, educators) to dispense among all people, various races, and religious groups to help promote the great humanitarian cause.

Brother Michael is born to his African American mother and his Puerto Rican father. He has lived his entire life as a Black man and has been viewed through the world as a

Black man, never fully accepted by the Latino community, mostly due to the primary features of a Black man and inability to fluently speak the Spanish language.

Dedication

I dedicate this masterpiece to my two children. May this body of work remind you when I am no longer on this planet Earth that your father had the best intentions to make the world a better place and help cure the misfortunes of Black Americans.

To my haters and the people that wished me harm. May this masterpiece relieve you of your self-hate, wickedness, and knaveries.

In remembrance of my two sidekicks Roco & Xena.

Acknowledgments

My mother **Gwendolyn** and father Ernest for giving me life and providing me with a life full of abundance.

Specifically to my mother, thank you for choosing an HBCU instead of me selecting a P.W.I.

Professor **Dr. Poe, Professor Benin,** and **Professor Walker** for providing me with my first teachings of black history.

The Black Conscious Community, you *brothers and sisters* have helped me in every aspect: health, self-esteem, and knowledge.

To all the participants who took the time and answered the questionnaire during the period when formulating this manuscript was not opaque.

Nava Goodman – I owe great apperception to you for always being there for me in my time of need. My line sister, Lincoln University classmate, close friend, you are the true definition and example of what a sweetheart is and the standard of a woman of that crimson and cream.

Lea Dominica – You once said to me I was heaven-sent. You have given me the confidence and forward-thinking of a man once battered and bruised.

Andreas Benjamin – A brother whom you can always call with long gaps in between.

The Inclusive One – For his mentorship, oversight, and compassion.

To all the **Freelancers** who took the time to accept this work. Without your assistance, this piece of literature that brings light to my people who have never been able to reclaim their birth rights, the opportunity to do so wouldn't have been a reality. Thank you so much for the extended hand.

Preface

T***his Is Going To Hurt – The Truth Always Does*** was written to bring heated debate topics to the forefront of the "so-called" Black communities throughout the United States of America. Constructed for all levels of literacy to indulge in the conversations, many of the subjects discussed in this book are to rattle the heads of the afraid, complacent, and oppressed people of these "so-called" Black communities. Black Americans' time for being apologetic for their misfortunes needs to come to an immediate cease-fire. ***This Is Going To Hurt – The Truth Always Does*** will do that!

The journey in creating this masterpiece was first conceived from the unprecedented events a person endures from living in the largest populated city in the world, New York City.

Living only minutes from the projects, the author was able to experience firsthand at a very young age the stricken conditions the Black race in the United States of America are truly living in. Contrarily, living in an upper-middle-class neighborhood toward the end of his high-school years, the astonishment of how other people lived there was unbelievable.

This entire book was designed to bring history, conducted research, and the hard truths of Black Americans together. Every section of discussion that has been presented in this book is important; breaking the chains of servitude is the king of the hill. Black Americans in the United States have always gotten the sh*t end of the stick, the last piece of toilet tissue on the roll.

Disclaimer

This book contains information gathered from many researched sources. All information is published for your reference and not as a substitute for any medical, legal, or financial advice. Neither the author nor the publisher is engaged in rendering any information in the capacity of a qualified or licensed professional. The author and publisher disclaim any personal liability for the information presented in this book. The material provided in this masterpiece is meant to supplement the various discussions. This information is like a broken key trying to fit into a door that does not exist. I am just a Black man in the United States of America trying to contribute to society.

Little Ni**az Turned Gorilla

(Background noise from the television) :

"A Staten Island man was killed today by officers of the NYPD. The officers allegedly involved are currently on paid administrative leave as a full investigation is now taking place." – 6 P.M. Local News

Reports

Just A Few Brother Talking:

Elzhi: These police killings of Black people need to STOP! This is what happens.

Cormega: Nah, bro. It's this racist-ass system here in America that's keeping us in the condition where we are not made to survive.

Elzhi: Good point, bro. But it was most definitely the crack epidemic that the government surged crack cocaine into our Black communities.

Cormega: Huh? Black communities! What Black communities are you talking about? I ain't never lived in a *Black* community a day in my whole life! If you know of one, let me know!

Elzhi: Bro, you from Jungle Nailz. If Mariners Harbor is not a Black community, then I don't know what is.

Cormega: My brother, if you or me or anyone that looks like us is living in a so-called "Black community," then we would own the banking institutions, we would run the school system curriculum, dominate the law enforcement agencies, public offices, or give out the pills in these pharmaceutical companies. We do not influence any of these industries.

Elzhi: Damn, bro, that was deep. I never thought of all of this like that. So, what should we do?

Cormega: You sure you want to know?

Elzhi: Yea, bro!

Cormega: ***This Is Going To Hurt***

Elzhi: ***The Truth Always Does!***

Introduction

"We cannot cure the symptoms without acknowledging the disease."

—Tom Burrell

The journey of a Black person in the United States of America can be fruitful like a juicy peach on a hot summer day. On the flip side, it can also be cold and empty, like being at a funeral on a fall day in October. So, what exactly does this mean? We are human, right? Life happens!

Black people should be grateful and suck it up and stop complaining about slavery (often said by other races and ethnic groups).

"The Holocaust killed over six million people. You don't hear Jews complaining about that still."

—Unknown

Well, my brothers and sisters, this is a half-truth. Today, many of those Black Americans who are descendants of African American slaves are still demanding the *Forty Acres and A Mule* with other financial respirations that were promised to be given after the ending of the Civil War. The author of this book says to you and among the homies and sistas, "Hold yourself accountable, don't pass the buck! Take advantage of the rights and benefits of citizenship in this so-called 'Land of the Free,'- the United States of America."

However, keep in mind and your position of influence the 400 plus years of the ***Trans-Atlantic Slave Trade***, the stripping of your culture, and your native tongue in your inner and outward demeanor. Use that aggression that has been mutated into your DNA from generations ago to facilitate discussion and the advancement of knowledge and history onto your children, family, friends, and the misinformed.

> "Words are powerful- they lie, they reflect the truth, and they even form something between lies and truth, but mostly they lie. Black people are the people that everybody tries their lies out on."
>
> —Hake R. Madhubuti.

Without any doubt, Black people have been pimped all around the globe, up and down the 50 states of the United States of America. Dating back to when their ancestors hopped on and off the slave ships like the infamous *Brookes*, the model for "Tight Pack" or more viscously jettisoned like the slaves on the Zong (Zong Massacre 1781). Yes, your ancestors were forced to be chained up from neck to ankles! Forced to have sex with their best friend's wife while the husband was forced to watch. Left devastated while witnessing their child being sold in the "Great Slave Auction," also known as the "Weeping Time" to *Master* and live an entire life of bondage.

Society is a repeat offender against the Black race throughout this world. All the lifelines have been used up. The remedies or so-called movements (political, religious) have not appropriately solved the real problems of the so-called post-racial society in America. The election of President Barrack Hussein Obama of 2008 and the re-election in 2012 indicated the hate and resentfulness of how society truly felt with institutional racism and police killings of Black people increased.

Let us consider that in this day and age, with all the so-called liberations and laws throughout the United States to protect all Americans from hate crimes, there is still a manual in circulation looking to enslave Black people. *The Making of a Slave* was a speech made by Willie Lynch on the bank of the James River in the state of Virginia in 1712. The sole purpose of this speech by Willie Lynch was to give a blueprint to plantation slave owners on how to destroy and separate Black Americans. Unfortunately, Lynch's strategy was successful in demoralizing the Black man, Black woman, Black child, and their descendants (present day). Captivating their minds to bring a race fully under another's group control both physically and psychologically.

You, the reader of this book, may have been enlightened to such information, but most Black Americans are still enslaved mentally. This masterpiece, *This Is Going To Hurt – The Truth Always Does*, is needed in the hands of the same Black men, Black women, Black children, and their descendants (us today) who suffered from those genocidal teachings. Read literature from the scholars who came before you to liberate your mind of centuries of captivity. Only this will kill the roots of those weeds embedded in the dark part of your history, reversing the negative misfortunes that have been done to you and your ancestors.

How much more suffering and mortification do Black Americans have to endure before moving on and escaping the systematic social engineering of the mental scars of slavery? The persistent tendencies of United States citizens (non-Black) to continue to ignore and covertly oppress Black Americans will never change. Unless the psychological and self-study of the African is taught and practiced, the oppressed and oppressor of African slavery has mutated into the offspring of each group. Both the slave master and the slave have their own unique DNA of being either the oppressor or the oppressed.

Before you question me, the author, if I am teaching hate throughout this masterpiece, you should ask yourself who taught you hate. Who are you really mad at, me or yourself? Abraham Lincoln, the 16th United States president, issued the Emancipation Proclamation that supposedly declared "that all persons held by slaves within the rebellious states are, and henceforward shall be free" over 100 years ago. But yet, today, the Black race in America is at the slowest rate setting up any businesses, industries, or job opportunities. Whether you are from N.Y. Philly, LA, Chi-Town, or the South, you are treated the same by society because you are Black. We all got the same problem. We all suffer the same oppression. You have been systematically taught to suffer peacefully.

The early history of the United States created two types of slaves. The etymology of the word "slave" derives from the tribes of speaking groups of people of central and eastern Europe who spoke Slavic. The captivity of this speaking group birthed the derogatory word "slave." This word has been bestowed upon Black Americans and is in the minds of walking day oppressors wishing to one day relive the days of their ancestors and have a personal slave.

Black slaves of the United States were categorized into two. The "House Negro." The one who loved his master (oppressor). This house Negro lived in the attic or the basement of the slave master's house. The house Negro was inseparable from his master and the master's plantation. The so-called "Field Negro" was the slave that caught hell. The one who ate the leftovers of that wild swine, pig feet, chitterlings (intestines), and pig ears. This slave hated his master. The field Negro was subjected to inhumane conditions and circumstances like living in shacks or huts. These so-called field Negros hoped for the demise of the master.

Both of these slaves exist in the present day. Which one are you? The house Negro or the field Negro? The majority of Black people in the United States are the so-called field Negro by default. Uneducated, afraid, living in that shack or hut (the projects of today). Well, guess what? Your argument isn't an argument; this isn't up for discussion. Pick a side, the house Negro or the field Negro. The Black race has yet to create a new identity as a people in this nation of the United States as previously done by the Black Panther Party (BPP) and the Nation of Islam. This standpoint was meant to make you feel unsettled.

How much more suffering do you want to keep enduring after already going through more than 400 years of bondage.

> *"My brothers and sisters, we have to put a stop to this, and it will never be stopped until we stop it ourselves."*
>
> —*Malcolm X*

I have worked many days and nights constructing, mapping, envisioning how to create the best way to decode this curse rooted upon the Black race in America. I am sick and tired of being sick and tired of my race and ancestors. We are a group of people on stolen land punishing one another that look just like each other. If you have eyes, you should be able to tell who is hurting each other in a face-to-face battle—the ones who look just like you. We style for free. Ask the Jordans, Jameses, Jacksons, and Jeffersons. We forgot about the old us (kings and queens) balling off the block for Master. *This Is Going to Hurt*, and this truth will, with a calculative reactive space of an adversary role.

However the facts are discussed or disputed, Black Americans have to be the sole group to strengthen the Black race character, culture, and heritage. The creation of the African slave had centuries to develop the result we currently see today of Black Americans. A race of people who have been misled, bamboozled, and deceived. The term "made in America" should be applied to all Black Americans just like a barcode on a product.

> *"Telling the truth and making someone cry is better than telling a lie and making someone smile."*
>
> —*Paulo Coelho*

Your average Black American should be classified as well-intentioned but incorrect, erroneously believing that the lives they are living are correct. Determining the morality of actions that they have been instructed to do so by the oppressors, parents, grandparents, tradition, and so willfully choosing to carry them out. This includes but is not limited to spending frivolously on materialistic items, i.e., Nike Air Jordans, designers, cars, jewelry.

Accepting government assistance for decades at a time added with poor food selections passed down from the enslaved ancestors eating the scraps like swine can be interchanged dozens of times. The main message intended is lifestyle choices. Lifestyle choices lead to being first place at the bottom of the social class globally.

More dangerous are the Black Americans that should be classified as the psychopaths of the Black race kamikazes with no intended purpose but their own. The drug dealer sells poison to the people, creating huge pain and substance abuse deficits. The gangbanger uses the codes of the streets (i.e., no snitching, preying off the weak and defenseless) to create a climate of fear and an environment of warfare among Black Americans state to state, coast to coast.

You gangbangers should be eradicated on sight!

You individuals consciously recognize the immoral implications of your actions and decisions and choose to continue an onslaught of nefarious atrocities.

During the unswerving time of being oppressed by the slave master, your ancestors were physically beaten, raped, castrated, and forced to accept a life of bondage. The tongue was forcibly removed out of your ancestors' mouths for learning to read and write the English language. Later on, in history, the descendants of the slave masters, such as the Allens, Browns, Hamptons, Jacksons, Jameses, Jeffersons, Johnsons, Joneses, Kings, Washingtons, just a few common names to be placed on Black Americans of present-day corporations and banking institutions, should be bestowed with the undisputed championship title of "moral culpable."

The gold standard of subjugation is to determine that slave masters and their descendants are the ones at fault and are to blame for the enslavement and destruction of Black civilizations globally. Yes, this is the truth, but this upcoming blanket statement is very pretentious. Today in the 21st century, the slave masters and their descendants are not the direct culprits opposing and subjugating Black people day to day with killings, kidnappings, rapes, and thefts. The moral culpability has shifted to ourselves, ultimately at fault for our commissions of harmful actions and losses to one another, bringing those results of pain to the manifestation of Black people's reality. The oppressors are more morally culpable, but we are also currently morally culpable. Both are to blame. The matter of opinion is up for discussion but will remain at an impasse till results change. Determining this answer is opaque.

The time has come to accept the era Black Americans live in. There is an overwhelming abundance of information available at your fingertips. This truth being ignored is not an option. It's a willful decision that Black Americans are making, and as a result of this decision, ignorance is here to stay and run amok for future generations to endure. Ignorance in this discussion should be defined as knowing even though necessary information is present because that information has been willfully refused or disregarded. Our truth is present. It's now a mental war within our minds of receiving the presence of truth by stopping to ignore the truth. To achieve prosperity as a people, we must first address and strategize these several topics here in this book, starting with *Economic Sovereignty.*

Chapter 1

Economic Sovereignty

"Wealth inequity and inappropriate behavior are the two most fundamental problems facing Black Americans."

—Claud Anderson, Ed.D

How far do you think the Black American dollar circulates throughout the so-called "Black communities" within the United States? I can tell you through direct conversations with Black Americans from all levels of the Black race, educated-uneducated, rich or poor, or far in between, that no one truly knows the answer. The exact number is extremely difficult to quantify.

What can be explained is that Black Americans have little to no control of their ***Economic Sovereignty.***

So, let's get straight to the point and properly discuss the importance of this chapter's title, "Economic Sovereignty." *Black* Americans primarily suffer from a lack of economic sovereignty, which is how we buy, sell, or produce in the context of being a consumer. Black Americans lack control of their finances within the community that can propel empowerment. The U.S. dollar may circulate 30 times or more in Black populated communities before it leaves and goes out of these so-called *Black* communities.

Interestingly enough, Black Americans indulge in a spiritual exchange before a transaction can even be conducted from within the Black community. For example, if a Black American doesn't trust another Black American, he or she doesn't buy from that person. If trust isn't first established in being consumers, as stated previously (buying, selling, and producing), transactions will not occur between them. Institutions aren't created, encouragement doesn't occur, and simply self-sufficient communities don't get built. Let's use the scenario of a high-school prom—junior and senior prom. More often than not, when these high schoolers search for their prom dresses and suits, they usually purchase their tuxedo or prom dresses from other races. The flower banquette, even the limo, is rented outside of the so-called Black community. Very small in everyday living but monumental in the economic prosperity this event creates for races other than Black Americans.

Black Americans who have the constitutional right of the liberties for being born in the United States of America based on the 14th amendment to be Americans have been ostracized. Sovereignty, you probably have been taught wrong on this definition. Sovereignty means that you are in control of the circumstances within the confines of your environment. *Economic Sovereignty* further dictates that you have established a marketplace at the subject of your discretion. Having this knowledge of the law gives you the backing of acquiring jurisdiction, owning land storefronts, property, etc.

Ultimately, establishing your *Economic Sovereignty* is saying some things without speaking. Understanding the rules of engagement (law) jurisprudence. Black people can cater to their needs and interest. Creating a paradigm of an existence that we want to exist in. When Black Americans as a whole with shared interest and abundance will make every financial decision easier. If Black Americans want to open a new high school, for example, each African American of the community can have the money to contribute the funds that are at their disposal to do so.

Black populated areas can achieve the prestigious title of a "Black Community" like the Freedom Colony, Greenwood District, in many ways. I have designed the model below, Figure 1: Peace or Pieces, to display through semiotics, which is a key tool one should possess to ensure the intended meaning of a sign or image.

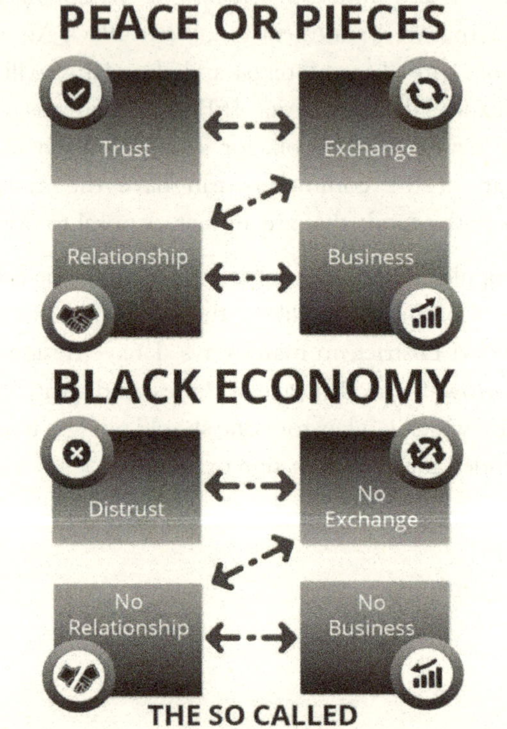
PEACE OR PIECES
Trust
Exchange
Relationship
Business
BLACK ECONOMY
Distrust
No Exchange
No Relationship
No Business
THE SO CALLED
"BLACK COMMUNITY"

FIGURE 1

Black Americans who are consumer-minded first, opposed to a seller-minded first, will take long and short commutes outside Black populated areas, whether by car, bus, taxi, or rideshare (Uber, Lyft, etc.) to shop for merchandise. This occurrence of transactions, when executed by millions of Black Americans, drastically depletes the money flow within these populated areas.

Economics transcends the U.S. dollar; the main objective for Black Americans in the United States of America should be to build wealth, not to say that money rules all and is more important than anything else. However, raising financial literacy in the Black community can facilitate growth. Raising this financial literacy needs to be taught so economic sovereignty can be established and gain control of the U.S. dollar. If more economic freedom was in the possession of Black people, the Black race would be able to have more time to travel, which facilitates creativity, have more time to raise their children, and establish institutions. I stress again that having more financial freedom—*Economic Sovereignty*—will give you more time in life other than working long hours plus overtime to keep material items such as a house, car, or liabilities that will be taken from you if you don't work.

In the so-called Black communities, the truth about economics is that Black Americans collectively are extremely rich and wealthy. Super rich to be more literal, worth hundreds of billions of dollars to state the least. Every year, the Black race makes the Koreans, Italians, and Middle Easterners multimillionaires. Have you ever wondered how all the so-called foreigners come to the United States and become so well off financially and economically in such a short time (approximately three to five years)? The Black American makes that reality economically viable.

Black Americans' ability as a community to make its own decisions concerning solely their resources and productivity is little to none. The battlegrounds of the United States of America are not united when it comes to race in particular. Nearly every race of people in the United States has economic sovereignty by sorting their goods and services, producing trades from their particular region: Chinatown, Little Italy, and Little Havana.

If the question was to be asked to a Black American walking down the street, "What are the five socio-economic factors?" let alone, "What is socio-economics?" you would most likely get a response of confusion and disarray. The fault of not knowing this answer is not of the Black American. It is the failed teachings of society not formally teaching Black Americans the basic life skills of survival. The lessons of the school of hard knocks forced Black Americans to learn, if lucky enough, the importance of occupation (career selection), education, income, real estate, and wealth.

So, what example or model do Black Americans have to follow and execute to implement economic sovereignty? For starters, it is not from our ancestors, due to outside influencers like crack cocaine. The majority of the history told to Black Americans is a history of slavery and bondage. Black Americans are so far behind on identity that the majority cannot pinpoint the original origin of their bloodline. That dismal situation leaves Black Americans with the objective to find, analyze, and observe the top group that is innately good with money.

The Jewish community, which networks extensively and loves one another, is all devoted to advancing one another's interests. The Jewish community does not focus on what they want to do individually; they focus on a service for the people's needs. Jewish people will not open a barbershop in the neighborhood when they know there is already a couple in the community. The Jewish community diversifies its services on what there is a current need for within the community. This particular community teaches connectedness; the making of wealth comes from other people's services. The correlation between financially successful people and those who struggle is the number of people you associate with.

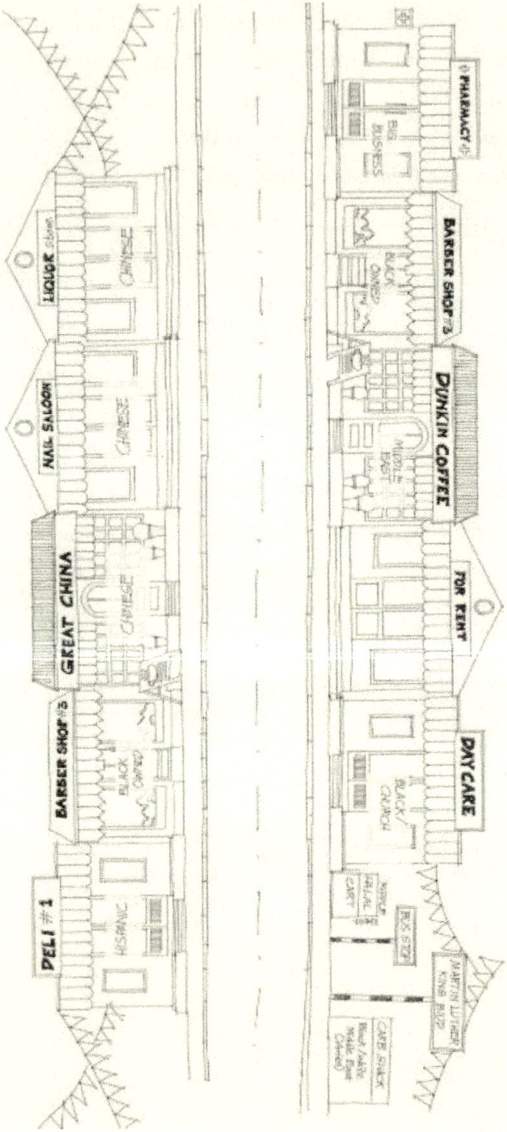
PHARMACY
BIG BUSINESS
BARBER SHOP #3
BLACK OWNED
DUNKIN COFFEE
MIDDLE EAST
FOR RENT
DAY CARE
BLACK CHURCH
FALAFEL CART
BUS STOP
MARTIN LUTHER KING BLVD
CAFE SHACK
LIQUOR store
CHINESE
NAIL SALOON
CHINESE
GREAT CHINA
CHINESE
BARBER SHOP #3
BLACK OWNED
DELI #1
HISPANIC

Figure 2.

The figure reveals how the few Black-owned businesses in Black populated areas lack business diversity amongst their Black entrepreneurs. Unlike Jewish communities, Black entrepreneurs will create several businesses in the same category, such as barbershops, beauty salons, etc. Having business diversity will create healthy competition between business owners in the same area, which can be great for creating a booming communal Economic Sovereignty. This business diversity creates competition that boosts innovation among businesses and spurs the invention of new or better products. Business diversity invites innovation, which ultimately benefits consumers with new and better products and services, helps drive economic growth, and increases living standards.

The stage is set for other races of people to set up shop and create businesses in the voids throughout Black populated areas. Since we need certain services and products to maintain our standard of living, Black people's lives become dollar bills to the eyes of other races. Oddly, since they need your money, you would think they would value your life and your respect. Instead, you get treated like garbage. You are presented with top-of-the-class services with glass barriers, bulletproof windows, no personable relationship. Ask your nail salon technician, hairdresser, or local liquor store associate if they know your name. It's not too much to ask of a customer that's been loyal for years supporting and paying money to a business and even tipping. We survive every attempt to discountenance us. We are treated this way because they don't value us. Your life should be valued more.

Hasidic Jews Can Do It, So Can We!

> "Excuses are the tools of the incompetent, which builds monuments of nothingness, those who indulge in excuses are…" —EE

In the year 2020, when many Black Americans felt like they could not get out that barrel and just complained, never get anything solid finished resembling a starting and establishing a self-sustaining community, Hasidic Jews on the other side of the isle of Monroe, New York, Orange County, broke the chains of a disagreement and feud of their misfortunes and established the Town of Palm Tree. This newly erected town in Orange County was the first new community established in the entire state of New York in 40 years. The last town created in New York was established in 1981, East Rochester.

These Hasidic Jews had a beef with the municipality of Monroe, New York. So, what do you think these Jews did about their current mishaps? They got busy! They organized, formed committees, townhalls, and came together as a community of like-minded individuals. Proceeding with the legal process of legislation of the land and the referendum of their land winning with an overwhelming number of votes that got the state bill signed by New York Governor Cuomo, creating their new town.

The second example for Black Americans to examine is the Mexican population in the United States. Americans in the United States have constantly joked about the Mexican that works for anything and will get the job done for super cheap. That "Mexican" in the United States has a hustle that should be applauded rather than mocked. Whether their citizenship is legal or illegal, they strive to work hard to support their families and communities. Mexicans have similar struggles to Black Americans, facing the barriers of institutional racism, insensitivity from the majority, and low social-class status.

Mexicans in the United States have built communities in which their people create the narrative for their race and culture (institutions, banks, police departments, etc.) They have built grocery stores to feed their communities and keep their native food readily available. Mexican Americans are widely said to work for anything to feed themselves and their family doing the jobs that most Americans, Black, white, and in-between, do not want to do. Cocal Landscaping is a premier example of a Mexican American business that provides temporary jobs for their people in their native land. Cocal Landscape, in Denver, Colorado, is a landscaping business that helps Mexicans from Mexico gain visas to the United States, which helps them and their family financially.

Greenwood District, Tulsa Oklahoma

Segregation has always been the backbone of American society. The early 1900s was no different. Tulsa, Oklahoma, was the epicenter for the Black American who visioned American optimism: "Life, Liberty, and the Pursuit of Happiness." Becoming known to the county as the Greenwood District, Black Americans took adversity upon themselves to rise against racial segregation and establish a nationally renowned Black entrepreneur community. This segregation inadvertently created a self-sustaining economy and birthed the world-famous throughway "Blackwall Street."

Without any doubt, the Greenwood District of Tulsa, Oklahoma, was no "So-Called Black Community." This was an example of what any foreign, outcasted group of people could accomplish. This Black populated district of people established thriving businesses. For example: The Law Firm of Spears, Franklin & Chappelle, Dreamland Theatre, owned by John Wesley Williams and his wife Loula Cotton Williams, Sowing Shop by Emma Buckner, hotels, libraries, food markets, and real estate agencies to help Black Americans establish their businesses, schools, medical facilities. Everything needed to be a certified self-sufficient community.

> "The fact that we remain as consumers and labors, rather than manufactures, planners, and managers, has a lot to do with the sense of inferiority." —Na'im Akbar

Black Americans go and establish relationships with all walks of life to become well-rounded people. A divided community will persist if Black Americans are incapable of identifying and addressing the most common problems of the whole community versus justifying their separate misfortunes.

Each Black person must make a conscious effort to free their minds of the inferiority of another race but their own. Call it what you want. Black people are like a chocolate chip cookie balled up in your hand, crushed, then sprinkled around the globe; call it the great Black diaspora. The Black American is conditioned not to put faith in another brother or sister's business.

This goes the same for Black-owned businesses. The fact that there are so few Black businesses is another issue. Remember, free is not always good. The real benefit of Economic Sovereignty won't be accomplished if we as a people always expect to receive services from another brother or sister for free or off the "strength." In fact, businesses grow when friends and families pay for your services first before it leaves the community. It is unacceptable to request or take services from Black businesses for free. Take a real deep thought about what is about to be argued. How do you expect a Black business owner who is most likely not inheriting this business and starting from the ground up to succeed when services are rendered for free? How is this unstable, unproven entrepreneur expected to pay his or her bills, support their family, or facilitate any type of financial growth, when a Black brother or sister comes around every time for a freebie? That form of action should be terminated on sight!

> "We the Black people assembled in Detroit, Michigan for the National Black Economic Development Conference are fully aware that we have been forced to come together because racist white America has exploited our resources, our minds, our bodies, our labor. For centuries we have been forced to live as colonized people inside the United States, victimized by the most vicious, racist system in the world. We have helped to build the most industrial country in the world."
>
> —The Black Manifesto (April 1969, a National Black Economic Development Conference meeting in Detroit)

We have already built several nations throughout man's existence. To keep it more recent, we built the United States through forced labor. So, why now should Black men and Black women continue to live in experimental establishments called projects? For the same reasons your Black American History is not taught to you from a young age. So acts like all the Black massacres can one day be repeated:

Colfax Massacre (Louisiana) 1873

Draft Riot (New York) 1863

The Clinton Riot of 1875

Ocoee Massacre (Florida) 1920

Rosewood Massacre (Florida) 1923

Chapter 2

Child Support Hurts The So-Called "Black Community" More Than It Helps It!

"Then Truth Might Hurt, But It's Always Helpful."

—Unknown

If you have not done so already, check out the section of this book, "Little Ni**az Turned Gorilla." I will briefly follow up on that dialogue between the two brothers in which one of the brothers was extremely upset that police officers were killing Black men. The shooting of Walter Lamar Scott is a dreadful example of what the brother was speaking about. A former United States Coast Guardsman, Walter Scott, was an unarmed Black man that was shot and killed while fleeing from former police officer Michael Slager of the North Charleston Police Department. On April 4, 2015 (now convicted of the murder of Walter Scott for Deprivation of Rights Under Color law), Slager executed Walter Scott. It's reported by court documents that Scott owed $7,000 in child support payments (arrears), and a bench warrant for his arrest had been issued. In Scott's case, the open bench warrant was a "Capture Dead or Alive" memo. This fatality could have been any Black man in America on child support on any given day. My brothers, just because it was not you does not mean it cannot be you next.

Figure 3.

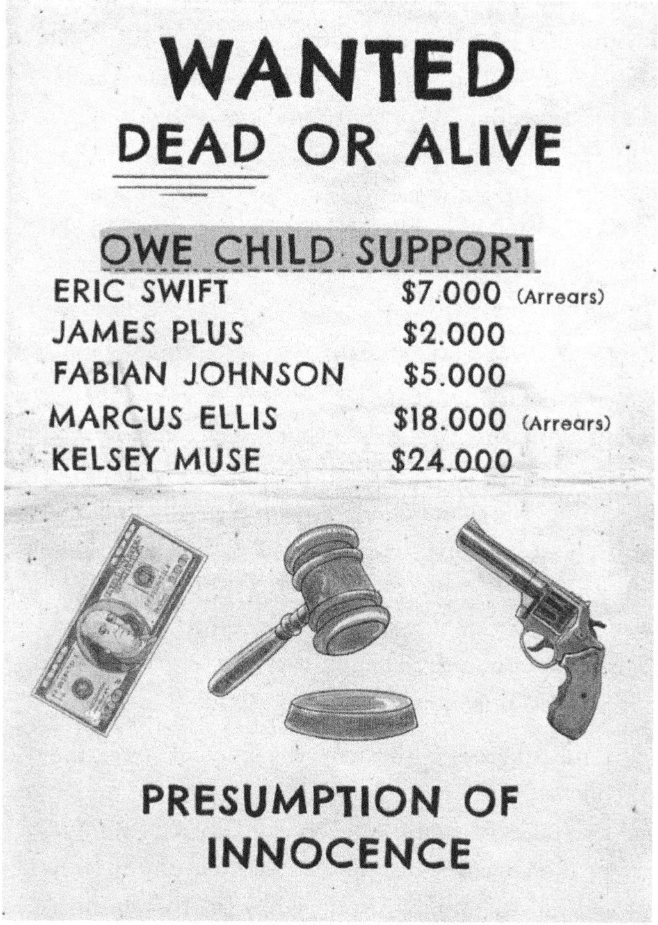

My intent for this chapter is not to make this a bashing section of either the Black man or the Black woman. However, my primary intent is to bring to light the subjugation of how child support dismantles the Black family, whether those parents are married or not. There are plenty of able-bodied Black parents capable of functioning in a civil manner to co-parent their child or children if local governments were not involved and used the warfare of child support to create an everlasting beef between the two Black parents. Walk with me in this chapter from a mindset of empathy rather than apathy. Only then will you fully understand and internalize how child support hurts the "so-called Black communities" more than it helps them.

According to the Pennsylvania Child Support Enforcement Program, the money accumulated each month from the parent ordered by the court to pay child support is used to supposedly pay for food, clothing, and other things for their child. Now, this may be the case for some honest people in the so-called Black community. More times than none, this child support money is not being used for its intended purpose. Instead, this money is used to support drug habits, vacations abroad, shopping sprees, or simply no initiative to get a job.

Currently, there is no system to adequately track the use of child support money spending. This current frenzy and fad that takes place in all the so-called Black communities across the United States means that the plaintiff receiving this so-called support can do whatever they want to do with the money every month without any type of tracking system to see if the money is being used for the child or children. The state defines this as food, clothing, and other things for their child. Brothers and Sisters, this is a problem, and it is one of the main reasons child support hurts the so-called Black community more than it helps it!

Image working 80 hours plus overtime each week for months and years just to see your paycheck garnished before your hard-earned money hits your bank account. Then you see a picture on social media of your child's parent on a vacation trip when you know that person has no job or any other source of income but child support. This is all too common in the so-called Black communities across the United States. This form of psychological warfare was solely designed to specifically equip the Black woman to play the role of mother and father to the child and eliminate the important role of the father in Black families, creating the ultimate form of self-hate and division.

"You and I are done! I'm putting your a** on child support" (the future plaintiff). Many Black people hear those gut-feeling words uttered way too frequently. Most people in relationships know that child support is one argument or break-up away. Child support is so heavily propagated in the media and everyday talk that it is the easiest way out and even a come up for some Black folk. So, let's take a step back and dissect the ramifications of the defendant once a child support claim has been opened with the state.

The first letter scheduled hearing from your county, city, or state court notifying you that legal proceedings have been brought against you to appear for an order of court support is a critical situation from the start. The Domestic

Relations of Montgomery County, Pennsylvania states on your order of court letter (All In Caps):

"IF YOU DO NOT APPEAR IN PERSON, THE COURT MAY ISSUE A WARRANT FOR YOUR ARREST AND YOU

MAY BE COMMITTED TO JAIL."

This is the first action of child support enforcement measures brought against you before you can hire an attorney or plead your dissent. Both parties, the plaintiff and the defendant, receive this letter of notification, but only the **defendant** is subject to this contempt of court. So, if this break-up, separation, or planning of warfare by the plaintiff has been initiated, the plaintiff has been greatly empowered to do you in by this tone and enforcement by the court.

At this point, things have already heated up between the two parties even before the defendant has even made their first court appearance. Unbeknown to the defendant, the plaintiff has already been offered children's health insurance coverage, immediate cash assistance, and food stamps by the state.

It is said by many that it's a man's world, but women run the world. When the Black woman chases that dollar (child support), she is crippled on her knees, disabled from achieving her destined potential. The Black man is chasing the Black women held back by lust and the systemic design to separate him from the Black woman. Black women have all the keys to the door, but both the Black man and women currently live in this nation of the United States inferior to their oppressors. The oppressor had centuries to figure all this out about you. Control the Black woman through materialism, which will control the Black man's lust—mind control.

The welfare state of Black families in America and its "happenstance" that Black females and their dependents are allotted benefits at the expense of losing the Black man. Black women are given assistance—money, healthcare, etc. The main stipulation to come upon these welfares is that no men can be present in the home. The implication is that the annihilation of the Black man's role shows through his masculinity, resulting in him feeling like a boy or young child.

The Black family's foundation of a healthy way of life is the arteries throughout the tree of life for us Black folk. Not having this strong family bond between the husband and wife is the recipe for an unstable family that will destroy the Black race. The negroid ancestry survived centuries of strenuous work and oppression since we could produce offspring at a higher success rate than any other race.

Child support creates the feeling of emptiness and loneliness, and the Black man sees vengeance and, more often than not, an unstable mindset of revenge. At its worst, violence and aggression sometimes build over toward the Black woman, demeaning the parenting needed to be there for the child or children.

Black Americans at one point had the vindication not to think and care what the world thought, but now, we should care more; it's time to figure it all out. Our ancestors lived the majority of their lives with all loss of hope without a happy ending. The conquerors control you; they control your mind, which controls your actions and decisions. Mind control is an act of war at a distance. Many Black people will never be aware this act of war is even taking place.

Child support was and is currently designed to destroy the Black family. The dissolution of Black *Economic Sovereignty* maliciously destroys any thriving in a Black community. The witnessing of killings of unarmed Black Americans by the police, to be seen over and over in media to cause traumatizing experiences. These are acts of war, which are preemptive strikes to keep Black people oppressed in the attempt to repel or defeat their oppressors from any imminent offensive or strategic advantage to come up from the bottom of the social classes.

Epigenetics is the study of heritable changes in mechanisms for gene expressions; this term will be used from this point and followed in Chapter 3, *Black Mother vs. Breastfeeding.* Embed this word and its definition in your mental rolodex (storing of information in your mind). Epigenetics, the changing of gene expression will occur by environmental factors, including systemic/institutional racism. In latent terms (hidden or concealed), epigenetics birthed the "Eugenic" way of thinking for the oppressors and conquerors. The so-called eugenic way of thinking, which differs, deals with the regulation (study) of the genetic activity of a cell. Eugenics is the manifestation of altering humans for a selective agenda.

The Making of a Slave by Jim Crow and Southern Democrat State Legislatures of the late 19th, early 20th, and 21st centuries used eugenics to alter the DNA of Black people. Harnessing undesirable epigenetics markers in Black Americans to reproduce fear of the oppressors and conquerors for future generations of Black Americans—actions of war fought at a distance.

Looking back at slavery for Blacks in America, stress unified on another. Presently, the stress of child support impedes the necessary skills to co-parent. Child support renders the debtor's health of paying child support payments the feeling of being fatigued, depressed, irritable, and, worst of all, becoming ill. This unnecessary stress from the child support mandated by the state, city, or local county, without any consideration or remorse, the stress child-support payments take a toll on both the mind and the body. The stress and pressure of making your child support payments on time or garnished from your paycheck can produce high levels of cortisol in the body, reducing brain functions. Inhibiting a happy, fulfilling life of balance and calmness.

Beautiful Black Queens, you are the real bosses; bosses in the family (home). The CEO that keeps the business (family) operational. You have to speak life into your

Black male partner, whether it is your husband or baby daddy. Beautiful Black Queens, understand this; Black men cannot fight the battles in America—corporate or in the streets and against you at the same time. Black men cannot fight home and fight the systematic systems in America. There has to be peace somewhere. A Black man's mind will not operate optimally if there is tension and war at home. This is how mistakes are made. The Black man will not stay home with his wife or baby mother if there is continuous turmoil.

Figure 4.

Beautiful Black Queens, you must help create an environment between the two of you. Being the bigger person, where there is love and peace. Where the Black man can be in your presence and the rest of the family and not feel pressured into leaving the house on any given day or at any given time. That late-night run or mid-day departure to escape drama will either cost that Black man his life legally (freedom) or six feet under the ground. Make home feel like how a home is supposed to be felt, welcoming. Beautiful Black Queens, you are the nurturers and the key to life; use your superpowers to heal and guide the Black man from turmoil and disarray.

Chapter 3

Black Mothers vs. Breastfeeding

"The More You Know Of Your History, The More Liberated You Are."

—Maya Angelou

To each his own. This is a term I have come accustomed to following to ***This Is Going To Hurt – The Truth Always Does*** help better my frustration when I see or hear things I may disagree with profoundly. *This Is Going To Hurt – The Truth Always Does* gives me a mental break to step away from that mindset. It is my calling to help liberate Black Americans and restore the royalty of the Black queen. There is no coincidence that Black slaves breastfed other races' children throughout the world's history.

The phrase "The Best Things In Life Are Free," hugs, smiles, sleep, laughter, love, lasting memories are just a few examples. Black mothers add breastfeeding to that list. Chapter one, *Economic Sovereignty,* addresses finances in the so-called Black communities in the Land of the Free. Breastfeeding is a way Black Americans can save extra money to help facilitate savings for investments, emergency funds, travel, and the passing of generational wealth. One 20-ounce container of Enfamil this current year this book was written is approximately $27.98 plus tax roughly 1.35 per ounce. If you get three of these containers each month, the cost is approximately $83.94, not including tax. Multiply that by twelve months, which is approximately $1007.28 again, not including tax.

The calculated prices that were just mentioned are just for one family's baby or babies.

Nutritional "inspired" breast milk is what is promoted by all the major breast milk companies.

These manufacturers are making a profit domestically and globally off breast milk that you Black queens produce naturally.

Here is the ugly truth or the beautiful lie. Your conqueror, crusader, colonizer, the one who gave you smallpox, syphilis, HIV, supplied you with a formula to replace the natural breastmilk mothers produce. There is a budget of billions of dollars spent every year to keep you deaf, dumb, and blind. The track record of big business is not a righteous one. Some would argue this truth spoken is a conspiracy.

Hatred is taught. Have you ever wondered or taken the time to think where the term snitch or snitching was birthed from? It was created during the long cotton-picking days of slavery. When the slaves on the plantation, working that intensive labor from sunrise to sunset and that Black mother forced to breastfeed and nurture the slave master's child took the risk of fleeing this life of torment. If captured alive, that slave would suffer the ultimate fate of death. The snitch would expose the escaping slave by giving in detail the covert operation such as the use of the underground railroad, used by the bravest of Black slaves, and the assistance of freedom fighters.

Figure 5.

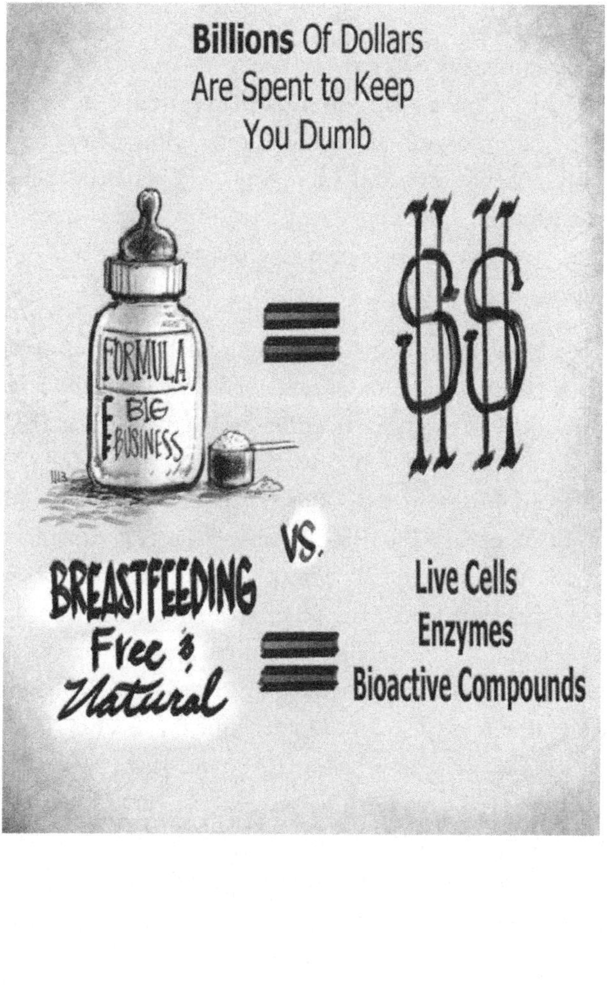

The image size of the top section, baby bottle, and the money sign are larger than the section beneath it to show how formula products backed by "Big Business" overshadow free and natural breast milk. The money spent to market the formula in comparison to educating Black mothers and Black fathers on breastfeeding is criminal. This capitalistic society produces the type of culture in which money is far more important than the well-being of women and children. Both the health of the newborn and the mother would benefit tremendously from breast-feeding. The newborn would receive live cells, enzymes & bio-active compounds.

How about a little history on breastfeeding before I debate with the naysayers of the breastfeeding community? Yes, breastfeeding is quintessential. Black slave mothers across the world were once forced to breastfeed by their slave masters. Blacks were not called ni**ers or coons, but Black mothers were specifically called "Wet Nurses." The primary duty of a wet nurse was to suckle another woman's child (the slave master's child). The failing school curriculum across the United States history is being told through the lens of the conquerors, leaving out significant events in our nation's past, thereby failing to go in-depth and teach the dark side of the United States' early conception. How can social studies and history classes leave out such a horrific duty as wet nursing?

Black slave mothers were forced into this position of employment, free employment in more realistic terms. The labor of breastfeeding was 100% free; no compensation whatsoever from the oppressor. This act of barbarity dates back at a minimum to the 1600s from the elite upper-class families of Europe and South America.

Many women slave owners did not want the work burden of breastfeeding. Sadly, Black mothers were separated from their children, never to see them again, and replaced with the slave owners' children. This shows that both the slave owner man and women actively participated in the harsh acts of slavery.

The Black women's maternal health of breastfeeding has a dark and heinous history of reproductive violence. Fortunately, wet nursing phased out, and women slave owners accepted the use of commercial formulas for their newborns' infants. However, formula companies falsely claimed or implied to mothers how inefficient the use of the formula is compared to a human mother's milk. The marketing ploys, such as newspapers, commercials, billboards, free starter packs, from federal, state, and local governments contributed to the declining breastfeeding rate of both the slave owner and Black mothers. As racial inequalities shaped the United States, Black mothers had to return to the workforce earlier than other races, leaving them with the decision to find a way to pump breastmilk, not usually allowed at job sites or the ability to breastfeed. The atrocious forcing wet nursing induced generational trauma, targeting both the physician and mental health of the Black mother. Slavery has altered Black people's body chemistry. Genetic markers were altered by traumatic experiences, creating the process of epigenetic changes.

Malnourished and fed the worst of foods, these Black slave mothers had to breastfeed another person's child, sacrificing their own child's nutrition. These elite upper-class families and slave owners noticed from the standpoint of jealousy and envy that Black infants were healthy and not dying as often as the slave owner and elite upper-class families' children because of their lack of breastfeeding, resulting in the birth of wet nursing and forced into overdrive, becoming extremely popular throughout the United States. The ramification of such experiences led to transgenerational trauma of breastfeeding in the lives of many African American women. Black Mothers VS. Breastfeeding.

New Black Mothers X Blinders

Breastfeeding is a proven natural part of the early parenthood process, just a mother and her baby. In the so-called "Black communities," Black mothers' cultural norm is not to breastfeed. In a study I conducted with various ages of Black mothers, the majority answered that they did not breastfeed over three months. This data rings the alarms on why breastfeeding and Black mothers made it into this book for discussion and why this truth must be made into meaningful and impactful dialogues to fix and liberate the so-called Black communities across the United States of America!

Generational blinders have been put onto Black parents. Blinders for the context of this particular conversation are hidden, lack of knowledge, unbeknown. Breastfeeding is what needs to be discussed more in the so-called Black communities. As a natural event and lifestyle, breastfeeding is supposed to be between the Black mother and her newborn. Breastfeeding education and empowerment from it is not being established throughout the parents' lives.

Build A Relationship With Your Baby From The Beginning!

What needs to be explained and taught to Black mothers is not just the importance of breast milk. It's the connection that you give to your baby being the first human relationship. As stated earlier, Black mothers breastfeed less than any other group. Enfamil, Similac, or any other baby formula, for example, other than natural breast milk, can probably get the job done at the poorest, non-nutritive level. But is that what you want for the precious newborn baby that took you nine months to produce? The bonding from breastfeeding, for starters, brings without a doubt an unmatched value of closeness and connection, ending the poor cycle of epigenetics of Black mothers not breastfeeding. Breastfeeding is the baby's first outside relationship. This small window of opportunity is key in establishing the main attributes of health and growth for this newborn.

"The Golden Hour"

This term, *The Golden Hour*, is not circulating in the houses of Black families when labor talks happen. This golden hour is pivotal to the bonding with the baby; within these sixty minutes, the mother and the baby should have uninterrupted contact to help the mother connect with the child, releasing hormones to instruct the uterus to contract and stop bleeding. This first hour of nursing improves the survival rate of the Black child and lowers the statistics of Black infant mortality. In fact, breastfeeding during the golden hour helps the mother breastfeed her child for a longer time.

A doctor, nurse, medical professional, or even the father sometimes is handed the newborn baby first. The American College of Pediatricians (ACPeds) recommends that the newborn be placed skin to skin with the mother. The first physical assessment of the newborn is conducted while on the mother's chest. This type of information needs to be discussed more importantly than the most recent episodes of love and hip hop if we as a Black race want to advance our race and reduce the last place statistic of medical data regarding breastfeeding.

First Couple of Days

The first several days after giving birth to your prince or princess, your body, Black women produces liquid gold "colostrum" fluid. Thick and yellow, this fluid is not yet considered to be milk yet; nevertheless, it has so many benefits for both you and your newborn. Starting with the newborn, colostrum fluid is packed with natural fats, proteins, antibodies, which are disease-fighting properties. Colostrum fluid goes into the ingestion gut of the newborn and becomes a layer of first defense which prepares for the breastmilk to arrive. Colostrum supports the immune systems, giving helpful bacteria to the lining of the intestines to fight against disease-causing bacteria. Approximately five days after giving birth, colostrum starts the transition into developing mature milk.

Colostrum is a powerhouse of rushing immune support, specific nutrients and white blood cells. The upper respiratory tract of the newborn is shielded from infections. Newborns are born to the world with low levels of antibodies, specifically secretory immunoglobin A, IGA for short. It is widely recognized by health professionals as the most vital immunoglobin the mother produces in her breast milk. There is no coincidence why the Black ancestry includes high cases of eczema in newborns. The correlation is parallel. The lack of breastfeeding stops immunoglobin formation that fights illnesses like eczema, wheezing, and milk allergies. Black woman, you produce a substance that is so precious and amazing that the properties can remain in your body long after breastfeeding is concluded.

Have you ever wondered what makes you fall in love with a person? What gives you butterflies in your stomach when a person you like or admire comes around? Makes the pupils in your eyes flare up so you can get more of an image of that person? You are under the influence of the hormone oxytocin. Nature develops hormones in your body which are instructions for the body. Oxytocin, which can be considered to be the love hormone, instructs the mothers to stimulate breastmilk from the breast. The mothering hormone oxytocin is pivotal for transmitting neurons to one another. The pituitary gland in the brain releases this oxytocin hormone to help both the baby and the mother, fostering love and developing that strong emotional bond.

Choosing not to breastfeed, you may see a missed opportunity. That missed opportunity of skin-to-skin contact between the mother and the child prevents the pituitary gland from releasing the oxytocin hormone that nature intended to do. This does not mean that if the mother doesn't breastfeed, she will not love or connect with her child. However, as a race of Black people, we cannot disregard this scientific data or call it pseudo.

Ultimately, the decision is yours, Black women. I say to you, with the highest level of respect without any hesitation over mind and matter whatsoever, that infant formula cannot duplicate, do better, or replace what you naturally produce. This is an absolute fact, my sisters. Changing the maternal diet of Black mothers, which research supports that breastfeeding prevents atopic dermatitis, AKA eczema. Your breastmilk contains three compounds that actively combats diseases like eczema, which is common in the Black lineage. A-tocopherol, B-tocopherol, and Prolactin increase your baby's immune system and reduce allergens. Mounting evidence supports this argument profoundly.

Internalize the information to help promote the welfare of Black American mothers. The mother's breast milk contains the best complex indigestible sugars to support the infant's gut health containing vital immune cells. The Americans Academy of Pediatricians has recommended that infants should be breastfed exclusively for the first six months of an infant's life, followed by age-appropriate foods until the infant reaches the age of twelve months old. For these reasons and more, the nutriments of breasting feeding are important.

Chapter 4

The Wrap-Up – Breaking The Chains of Servitude

Get Conscious. Your People Depend On It!

In this final chapter, I will give you several strategies to help you navigate the road to Black consciousness. Before you can begin this long journey into Black consciousness, you need to understand what Black consciousness truly means.

According to Bantu Stephen Biko, famously known to the world as Steve Biko, one of the founding fathers of the Black Consciousness movement in South Africa, Black Consciousness is an "attitude of mind" or "a way of life." This way of life consists of changing the oppressed mindset, to look inward and outward to construct Black liberation. By no means is this journey short nor easy. But first, the psychology of Black people must change along with spiritual liberation. As Haki R Madhubuti would say, "I use writing as a weapon offensively and defensively, to help raise the consciousness of myself and my people."

Follow The Leader

One of the main reasons so many people join organizations like the divine nine in the world is because they want to be around like-minded individuals. This should be your next step on this treacherous journey. Get yourself into a group, organization, or have a mentor who can help you on the right path to resources and information you may have never known existed. Just like 50 Cent, a Hip-Hop rapper from South Side Jamaica, Queens, New York, said during a rooftop interview, "My grandfather once told me: 'You'll only go as far as the people that you talk to for absolutely no reason.'" Needless to say, if you spend your time talking to people who can't offer you any information or resources to help better your life, then you are completely wasting your valuable time. This is why I strongly advise that you surround yourself with like-minded individuals.

Burn The Snakes - Controlled Opposition

According to the Urban Dictionary, a controlled opposition is a protest movement led by government agents. While this definition may be very true in many instances, this movement is exercised by religious leaders, gang leaders, organization leaders, or heavily followed individuals to promote propaganda. For example, propaganda that is commonly used is "don't you go working for the white man," but contrarily, this person, group, or organization may covertly accept money in the form of a grant, loan, charity, or some other form of funding to establish a business or nonprofit organization.

This sheisty behavior contradicts many of the slogans, mottos, and statements made by these people, groups, and organizations. Ultimately, this rhetoric is telling you not to live a productive legal life. Entrepreneurship is something I highly suggest for Black Americans. Nonetheless, getting your capital by committing crimes or doing consignment work to fund your business is not the route to go.

Become Fearless

You have been taught through double consciousness, which is knowing a lie while living in contradiction, that being Black is inferior to other races, human beings. This is the furthest from the truth. You are born from the bloodlines of Kings and Queens; Makeda, Queen of Sheba, Nefertiti, Queen of Ancient Egypt, Ranavalonna I, of the Hova Dynasty, Queen of the Kingdom of Madagascar, Shaka Zulu, King of the Zulu Kingdom, Southern Africa, King Tut, of Ancient Egypt 18th Dynasty (New Kingdom), Mansa Musa, Keita Dynasty of the West African Mali Empire. Do not be afraid to proudly wear your Blackness and melanated skin around the world.

Notwithstanding that the truth will hurt and hit you deep, you will be rejected! You will be labeled a menace to society! Negative racial stereotypes and their effect on attitudes toward Black Americans result from the current conditions we see today in America.

> "The racial stereotypes of early American history had a significant role in the shaping of attitudes toward African Americans during that time."
>
> —Laura Green.

Message To My Young Brothers and Sisters

You have so much potential to be great. A great learner is a great listener. Wake up every day and be the best version of yourself you can strive to be. Read books to empower yourself. Build a network of connections with people to increase your resources. The world is against you, but keep your energy golden and uplift those around you.

Go to a Historically Black College and University (H.B.C.U)! Nowadays, going to college is all about making a profit off of you, especially if you do not major in a technical degree such as engineering, medical, or information technology. If you do not measure in the aforementioned professional areas, do not plan on making a decent amount of money straight out of college. This is why I emphasize that you go to a Historically Black College and University. Take your talents and potential to any part of the United States with an H.B.C.U.

The personal experiences you can get at an H.B.C.U. cannot be glorified enough. The endless benefits are truly unmatched. For starters, the friends you will come across at an H.B.C.U. are unmatched. Your peers and classmates will be from a similar culture, similar plights, trials, and tribulations. At the end of the day, the H.B.C.U. experience is a family. Regardless of the section you decide, Howard University, Morehouse College, Hampton University, or the first-degree granting H.B.C.U. Lincoln University, each person in this network, lifts the other. This will propel you to different heights, opposed to you taking your talent and potential to a predominately white institution (P.W.I) and playing the role of a lone ranger. Surrounded by many people who do not share similar experiences and cannot relate to your life struggles will more often than not leave you feeling empty and alone.

To My Older and Wiser Brothers and Sisters

You need to better articulate the need for brotherhood, sisterhood, and family. That is what sustained the Black race in the darkest hours of slavery. Each Black slave had each other. Black Americans currently have lost that way and found themselves alone, scratching, clawing, just like that common saying "crab in a barrel mentality," trying to make it to the top all on their own. This way of functioning creates the daunting task of becoming successful.

Observance

So, what's stopping the chains of servitude from being broken by Black Americans in the present day? It's the several stumbling blocks still rooted in our nation's systems. The book *Institutional Racism A Primer on Theory and Strategies for Social Change* written by author Shirley Better is scholarly excellence in bringing to light the stumbling blocks of America's systemic racism. Right now, what can be done is address the enemy face to face: ourselves. Black Americans focus on problems rather than developing solutions. It is famously stated by Albert Einstein that "insanity is doing the same thing over and over again expecting a different result." No! Black people are not insane. However, if this current condition of Black Americans transcends to several generations into the future, then we as a people are indeed insane. To continue not to fix the problem and leave this mess to our descendants, a life of oppression, is genocidal.

Civic Engagement

Taking action to better the community while encouraging other community members to do the same act of service. This understanding of civic engagement is the building block of what a community needs. A very deep commitment to the collaborations of its residents. When its elders and leaders engage in this civil duty, communities strengthen. Civic engagement can fit so many different interests of a community resident, politics, education, law enforcement, health care, and social services. The only way civic engagement can work for Black Americans is if the everyday Black person, whether elderly or adolescent, shows compassion and courage within their community. Only then can a powerful force of a thriving Black-owned, Black-built, Black community be established.

We can aimlessly wander around the United States praying for a miracle, or as a people, we can identify a problem then execute a goal in fixing that problem. Configuring a plan, striving endlessly to complete it. Our ancestors left the blueprints of achievements throughout the world. The formula is to learn from their mistakes and conquer any complex problem that persists. I'm not beating around no bushes here; I am firing propositions and fire extinguishers through this book to put those fires out.

That Rabbit-Hole Deep

If you don't drop that love and Hip Hop mentality, your race will be left and dropped further down that rabbit hole. Every objective statement made in this book cannot be disputed or argued without any historical backing from each rival party. The advantage of having a historical backing or edification loads the shooter of an argument with a historical analogy, a preface for intellectual discussion. You, the reader or young adult who is thinking about money, clothes, turning up, and getting sum pu**y might firmly ask why you should invest your valuable time and energy in historical research. You say that "everyone knows that Africans were slaves and brought to America. Enough already with that slave shit."

Well, guess what? Hard times call for drastic measures like the codes of the streets you got to go it; they are not going to give it to you. That new jail that is forecasted for your Black brother and sister has not yet been built. This book here is a blueprint trying to equip you with a defense. This information I'm dropping is yet ever to be discussed and written in this manner and is now exposed to the world to see, digest, and ridicule. Watch the forces against your race, try to swiftly switch the plan before this book progresses in the hands of enough Black people. So, to answer your question about doubting researching historical facts, ask yourself this question: Why can't self-community empowerment be the code of something to learn? You, the reader, can make it happen for your Black-populated community full of thriving businesses, like the Greenwood District of Tulsa, Oklahoma, or continue to live and watch it happen for them like it has been for the last 400 centuries and counting. This life is full of consequences and penalties. Knowledge is the skill you need to play the game of life. Slavery, prisons sentences, transgressional oppression are the repercussions of a loss in that game of life.

Controlling The Narrative

The trending terms in recent years, *Melanin, Black Girl Magic,* has created an insurgence of prideful Black brothers and sisters with a higher sense and glow of empowerment of their race. This self-identification strengthens individuals, which establishes confidence fostering an environment of positive people. The spelling of words (casting a spell) has impactful effects on one's self or group.

Derogatory names such as quadroon, octoroon, negro, or ni**a are systemic ways of controlling the narrative of Black people. The controlling of a specific narrative establishes a story, an account of events, whether true or fictitious. Other races control the controlling narrative of Black Americans. Anytime there is a national disaster, mass shooting, or event, government officials and police departments use the power of narrative control to offset any conspiracy theories.

It wasn't until recently, 2013, to be exact, that the United States Census Bureau removed the disparaging word "negro" from surveys. This classification of Black people was more than just an outdated description in modern-day society. It was a form of controlling the narrative, a Jim Crow-era narrative.

Recognizing That A Problem Exists

Generations of Issues concerning Black Americans:

Economic Sovereignty (Economic Structure)

Child Support (Destruction of the Black Family)

Breastfeeding (Stripping of Culture)

Servitude (Mind Control)

1. Change happens in the mind foremost, followed by the heart and gut.

2. You, us, Black Americans, must care enough to know and put the information of truths into action.

3. Eradicate any possibility for denial. No change will succeed or take place in that state of mind.

*Remember, if there is a recession or pandemic such as COVID-19, Black Americans will get hit the hardest economically. Be advised cautiously. When a natural disaster occurs, Black Americans will undoubtedly get serviced last with aid like what the United States witnessed from Hurricane Katrina in August of 2005.

Etymology

Language is a science that Black people should master and study. Once again, the school system has failed you. The term etymology to Black people is a cluster of far-fetched signs and symbols. Indubitably, etymology gives a critical analysis of a word and reveals its real truth about its history. Black Americans cannot talk about their history through other races' languages. English, Arabic, Spanish, etc. Etymology is the key to understanding language. Use this power study to your advantage. Etymology is a divine faculty you have to invoke through the presence of the information your ancestors left for you in your DNA (epigenetics). Not knowing your history has left you unclear of your past, present, pain, and suffering, resulting in you not understanding how the conquerors control this world's political structure.

We as a people don't know the political structure of the United States. If you examine the United States Senate, you rarely see any Black representation in these elected positions. We will never move forward and be liberated from any Jim Crow if we cannot master this political system. Studying the origins of words will show you the birth of African history. The heart of a people is its culture and the language used by the people. When you study etymology, you will see our people's history in all major scriptures: The Holy Bible, The Holy Koran, etc. When language is put at the forefront of melanated people, you will discover a long, rich history, brazened in culture, not a history of self-hate, killings amongst ourselves across highlighted areas like Chicago, Illinois, Philadelphia, Pennsylvania, New York City, Los Angeles, and California.

Our scholars have not emphasized etymology, the study of language which birthed many of Earth's languages. The *Metu Neter,* the mother of all languages, this ancient language is where present-day society developed its culture from. Carl Linnaeus is the founding father of racism, scientific racism to be exact. He was the true racist that birthed the classification of the human species. When you read the words in this book, you must interpret them. Just don't read it at face value; interpret every word.

Little Ni**az Turned Gorilla

Elzhi: Got Dam! All that shit. It is what it is, I guess.

Cormega: Yea, bro. It makes you think, though. Who you really mad at? Me or yourself?

Elzhi: I know you're not done here. Keep going with the information.

Cormega: You know This Is Going To Hurt Even More!

Elzhi: I already know, bro. The Truth Always Does!

Appendix

Appendix 1.A. – *For Child Support Hurts The So-Called "Black Community" More Than It Helps!*

In the Court of Common Pleas of MONTGOMERY County, Pennsylvania
DOMESTIC RELATIONS SECTION

[redacted]
Plaintiff
vs
[redacted]
Defendant

) Docket Number:
)
) PACSES Case Number: [redacted]
)
) Other State ID Number:

ORDER OF COURT

You, [redacted] plaintiff/defendant of [redacted]
are ordered to appear at HOME BY REMOTE TELECONFERENCE [redacted]
before a conference officer of the Domestic Relations Section, on OCTOBER at 1:00PM for a conference, after which the conference officer may recommend that an order for support be entered.

You are further required to bring to the conference:

1. A true copy of your most recent Federal Income Tax Return, including W-2s, as filed;
2. Your pay stubs for the preceding six (6) months;
3. The Income Statement and the appropriate Expense Statement, if required, attached to this order, completed as required by Rule 1910.11 (c);
4. Net income from business or dealings in property;
5. All business tax returns with all schedules and attachments, if applicable;
6. Verification of child care expenses;
7. Proof of medical coverage which you may have, or may have available to you;
8. If a physician has determined that a medical condition affects your ability to earn income you must obtain a Physician Verification Form from the domestic relations section, sign it, have it completed by your doctor, and bring it with you to the conference.

   If you intend to offer the Physician Verification Form as evidence at any record proceeding, you must comply with the timeframes established by PA Rule of Civil Procedure 1910.29(b)(2).
9. Information relating to professional licenses, and.

Service Type M [redacted]

Appendix 1.B. – *For Child Support Hurts The So-Called "Black Community" More Than It Helps!*

[illegible] PACSES Case Number: [illegible]

If you fail to appear for the conference/hearing or to bring the required documents, the court may issue a warrant for your arrest and/or enter an interim support order. If paternity is an issue, the court shall enter an order establishing paternity.

THE TRIER OF FACT SHALL ENTER AN APPROPRIATE CHILD SUPPORT ORDER BASED UPON THE EVIDENCE PRESENTED, WITHOUT REGARD TO WHICH PARTY INITIATED THE SUPPORT ACTION. THE DETERMINATION OF WHICH PARTY WILL BE THE OBLIGEE AND WHICH WILL BE THE OBLIGOR WILL BE MADE BY THE TRIER OF FACT BASED UPON THE RESPECTIVE INCOMES OF THE PARTIES, CONSISTENT WITH THE SUPPORT GUIDELINES AND EXISTING LAW, AND THE CUSTODIAL ARRANGEMENTS AT THE TIME OF THE INITIAL OR SUBSEQUENT CONFERENCE, HEARING, OR TRIAL. IF SUPPORTED BY THE EVIDENCE, THE PARTY NAMED AS THE DEFENDANT IN THE INITIAL PLEADING MAY BE DEEMED TO BE THE OBLIGEE, EVEN IF THAT PARTY DID NOT FILE A COMPLAINT FOR SUPPORT.

BY THE COURT:

Date of Order: SEPTEMBER 1 2020 *PER CURIAM*

JUDGE

YOU HAVE THE RIGHT TO A LAWYER, WHO MAY ATTEND THE CONFERENCE-HEARING AND REPRESENT YOU. IF YOU DO NOT HAVE A LAWYER, GO TO OR TELEPHONE THE OFFICE SET FORTH BELOW. THIS OFFICE CAN PROVIDE YOU WITH INFORMATION ABOUT HIRING A LAWYER.

IF YOU CANNOT AFFORD TO HIRE A LAWYER, THIS OFFICE MAY BE ABLE TO PROVIDE YOU WITH INFORMATION ABOUT AGENCIES THAT MAY OFFER LEGAL SERVICES TO ELIGIBLE PERSONS AT A REDUCED FEE OR NO FEE.

LAWYER REFERRAL SERVICE

100 W AIRY ST REAR
NORRISTOWN PA 19401-4724
(610) 279-9660

AMERICANS WITH DISABILITIES ACT OF 1990

The Court of Common Pleas of MONTGOMERY County is required by law to comply with the Americans with Disabilities Act of 1990. For information about accessible facilities and reasonable accommodations available to disabled individuals having business before the court, please contact our office at: (610) 278-3646. All arrangements must be made at least 72 hours prior to any hearing or business before the court. You must attend the scheduled conference.

Service Type M Page 2 of 2 Form CM-508 02/20

[illegible]

Appendix 1.C. – *For Child Support Hurts The So-Called "Black Community" More Than It Helps!*

In the Court of Common Pleas of MONTGOMERY County, Pennsylvania

DOMESTIC RELATIONS SECTION

PO BOX 311, NORRISTOWN, PA 19404-0311-11

Phone: (610) 278-3646 SEPTEMBER **Fax:** (610) 239-9637

Plaintiff Name:
Defendant Name:
Docket Number:
PACSES Case Number:
Other State ID Number:

Please note: All correspondence must include the PACSES Case Number.

Social Security Number Disclosure Notice

In accordance with Section 7(b) of the Privacy Act, you are hereby notified that disclosure of your Social Security number is mandatory based on Section 466(a)(13) of the Social Security Act [42 U.S.C. 666(a)(13)], Pennsylvania Consolidated Statutes (Pa C.S.) §4304.1 and §4353(a.2). Additionally, you are notified that this information will be used by the Title IV-D program to locate individuals for the purpose of establishing paternity and establishing, modifying, and enforcing support obligations.

Service Type M

Appendix 1.D. – *For Child Support Hurts The So-Called "Black Community" More Than It Helps!*

In the Court of Common Pleas of MONTGOMERY County, Pennsylvania
DOMESTIC RELATIONS SECTION

[illegible]	Plaintiff	) Docket Number
vs		) PACSES Case Number [illegible]
[illegible]	Defendant	) Other State ID Number

Order

AND NOW to wit, this OCTOBER 2019 it is hereby Ordered that:

PURSUANT TO PLAINTIFF'S WRITTEN REQUEST CASE IS TERMINATED EFFECTIVE 10/22/19 PLAINTIFF FORGIVES ARREARS. FEE REMAINS DUE. UPON FULL PAYMENT OF FEE CASE TO CLOSE.

BY THE COURT:

Per Curiam

OCTOBER 2019
Date

JUDGE

Service Type M

Authors Notes

This Is Going To Hurt – The Truth Always Does, makes the argument that Chapters 1-4 are pressing issues of Black Americans that are not spoken about at cookouts and dinner tables, deeming the topics not to be important at all. My intended purpose is to contribute to the excellent scholarly work conducted by the ancestors and outside races to help bring light and liberation to Black folk worldwide.

The collage of Ebonics blended with the cheetah print design was first created to draw the attention of a younger, modern audience with the vision of having this book in the hands of the reader thinking and expressing a hunger for more information of what has to be offered from this distinctive image.

This book being my first publication, the learning curve was profound. Each and every day, I've gathered ideas, methods, and experience on how to create a book from just a thought. Whether it was learning the correct genre or properly categorizing my work, which consists of a unique style, drafting, revisions, and finding out how to create a book that includes many additions beyond words: ISBNS, printing, art designs, figures, and press releases, this list can be very long.

However, the process was very daunting but also very rewarding. The writing process is a beautiful system of morality. Thus, many challenges arose from this book's beginning, mainly a place of hurt and grief. Each chapter is very dear to my heart, and with these discussions, I am confident they will liberate my people, sparking their brains, which will change their misfortunes.

Economics and breastfeeding are topics that would habitually be beyond my reach of knowledge and expertise. However, if I had stuck to what I perceived these topics to be without venturing into new territory from a research perspective, my quality of work would have been less rich for argumentative debates.

Selected Bibliography

Africa.com. "Great Ancient African Queens," June 20, 2019. https://www.africa.com/great-Ancient-African-Queens/.

Anderson, Claud. *Powernomics: The National Plan to Empower Black America.* Chevy Chase,

MD: Power Nomics Corporation of America, 2001.

Associated Press. "Walter Scott Had Bench Warrant for His Arrest, Court Documents Show." NBC News, April 10, 2015. https://www.nbcnews.com/storyline/walter-scott-shooting/walter-scott-shooting-warrant-over-child-support-court-records-show-n339151.

Better, Shirley. *Institutional Racism: A Primer on Theory and Strategies for Social Change.* 2nd ed. Lanham, MD: Rowman & Littlefield, 2007.

Bey, Abdullah El Talib Mosi. *Moors and Masonry.* Philadelphia: Black and Nobel, 2016.

Biko, Steve. *I Write What I Like: Selected Writings.* Chicago: University of Chicago Press, 2002.

Black Enterprise Editors. "African American Economics: Real Facts." Black Enterprise, March 6, 2019. https://www.blackenterprise.com/african-american-economics/.

Blay, Zeba. "12 Words Black People Invented, And White People Killed." Huffington Post, October 19, 2015. https://www.huffpost.com/entry/black-slang-white-people-ruined_n_55ccda07e4b064d5910ac8b3.

Burrell, Tom. *Brainwashed: Challenging the Myth of Black Inferiority.* Carlsbad, CA: Smiley Books, 2010.

Butler, Sophia. "Child Support & Its Effect on the Black Family." The Black Detour, January 1, 2018. https://theblackdetour.com/child-support-black-family/.

Centers for Disease Control and Prevention. "What Is Epigenetics," 2020.

https://www.cdc.gov/genomics/disease/epigenetics.htm.

Charlamagne Tha God. *Black Privilege: Opportunity Comes to Those Who Create It.* New York:

Atria Books, 2017.

Fama, Jilian. "U.S. Census Bureau Drops 'Negro' From Surveys." ABC News, February 25, 2013. https://abcnews.go.com/Politics/OTUS/us-census-bureau-drops-negro-surveys/story?id=18591761.

Feis, Aaron. "Hasidic Jewish Community Creates NY's First New Town in Decades." New York

Post, 2019. https://nypost.com/2019/01/08/hasidic-jewish-community-creates-nys-first-new-town-in-decades/.

Forman, James. "The Black Manifesto." *National Black Economic Development Conference*, 1969, 7–11. https://episcopalarchives.org/church-awakens/files/original/c20bd83547dd3cf92e788041d7fddfa2.pdf.

Freeman, Andrea. *Skimmed: Breastfeeding, Race, and Injustice.* 1st ed. Palo Alto, CA: Stanford University Press, 2019.

Garner, Bryan A., ed. *Black's Law Dictionary.* 11th ed. Toronto: Thomson Reuters, 2019.

Gordon, Lewis R. *I Write What I Like: Selected Writings (Foreword).* Edited by Steve Biko.

Chicago: University of Chicago Press, 2002.

Green, Laura. "Negative Racial Stereotypes and Their Effect on Attitudes Toward African-Americans." Jim Crow Museum of Racist Memorabilia. Accessed November 22, 2021. https://www.ferris.edu/HTMLS/news/jimcrow/links/Essays/vcu.htm.

Height, Tatiana. "Analyzing Communities in Black America: How Urban and Regional Planners Can Plan for Prosperous Black Communities." *Community and Regional Planning Program: Student Projects and Theses* 47 (2017). http://digitalcommons.unl.edu/arch_crp_theses.

Introcaso, David. "Andrea Freeman Discusses Her Just-Published Book, 'Skimmed: Breastfeeding, Race and Injustice' (January 9th)." The Healthcare Policy Podcast, 2020. https://www.thehealthcarepolicypodcast.com/2020/01/andrea-freeman-discusses-her-just-published-skimmed-breastfeeding-race-and-injustice-january-9th-.html.

James, George G. M. *Stolen Legacy: The Egyptian Origins of Western Philosophy*. Eastford, CT:

Martino Fine Books, 2015.

Jan, Tracy. "A Landscaper's 'Hire American' Plan Ended with Bringing in Mexican Workers to Finish the Job." Washington Post, October 5, 2017. https://www.washingtonpost.com/business/economy/a-landscapers-hire-american-plan-ended-with-bringing-in-mexican-workers-to-finish-the-job/2017/10/05/f4656234-9743-11e7-b569-3360011663b4_story.html.

Johnson, Hannibal B. "Greenwood District." The Encyclopedia of Oklahoma History and

Culture. Accessed November 22, 2021.

https://www.okhistory.org/publications/enc/entry.php?entry=GR024.

Klein, Ernest. *Klein's Comprehensive Etymological Dictionary of the English Language*. New York: Elsevier, 1971.

Lynch, Willie. *The Willie Lynch Letter And the Making of A Slave*. African Tree Press, 2011.

Madhubuti, Haki R. *Enemies: The Clash of Races*. Chicago: Third World Press, 1978.

Meloni, Maurizio. "If We're Not Careful, Epigenetics May Bring Back Eugenic Thinking." Center for Genetics and Society, March 15, 2016. https://www.geneticsandsociety.org/article/if-were-not-careful-epigenetics-may-bring-back-eugenic-thinking.

National Archives and Records Administration. "The Emancipation Proclamation." Accessed November 22, 2021. https://www.archives.gov/exhibits/featured-documents/emancipation-proclamation.

NC Health News Editor. "Distant Echoes of Slavery Affect Breast-Feeding Attitudes of Black

Women." NC Health News, March 3, 2016.

https://www.northcarolinahealthnews.org/2016/03/03/distant-echoes-of-slavery-affect-

breastfeeding-attitudes-in-black-women/.

Office of Child Support Enforcement. "Child Support Handbook," 2013. https://www.acf.hhs.gov/sites/default/files/programs/css/child_support_handbook_with_t oc.pdf.

Pratt, Eleanor. "Child Support Enforcement Can Hurt Black, Low-Income, Noncustodial Fathers and Their Kids." Urban Institute, June 16, 2016. https://www.urban.org/urban-wire/child-support-enforcement-can-hurt-black-low-income-noncustodial-fathers-and-their-kids.

Rothstein, Richard. *The Color of Law: A Forgotten History of How Our Government Segregated*

America. New York: Liveright, 2017.

SHN Staff. "The 'Golden Hour': Giving Your Newborn the Best Start." Sanford Health, September 24, 2018. https://news.sanfordhealth.org/womens/pregnancy/the-golden-hour-giving-your-newborn-the-best-start/.

Tatum, Beverly Daniel. *Why Are All the Black Kids Sitting Together in the Cafeteria?: And*

Other Conversations About Race. New York: Basic Books, 2017.

Wikipedia. "Killing of Walter Scott." Accessed November 22, 2021.

https://en.wikipedia.org/wiki/Killing_of_Walter_Scott.

Williams, Chancellor. *Destruction of Black Civilization: Great Issues of a Race from 4500 B.C. to 2000 A.D.* 3rd ed. Chicago: Third World Press, 1992.

Windsor, Rudolph R. *From Babylon to Timbuktu: A History of the Ancient Black Races*

Including the Black Hebrews. Atlanta: Windsor Golden, 2006.

Upcoming Publications

INDEX

A

A-tocopherol, 58
AKA Eczema, 58
American optimism, 34
Angelou, Maya, 49
Ashmun Institute, 1
Atopic Dermatitis, 58

B

B-tocopherol, 59
Better, Shirley, 64
Biko, Bantu Stephen, 60
Black
  American History, 36, 63
  Americans, 14–25, 32–34, 62–69
  Americans' ability, 28
  Black woman, 15–16, 41–44, 53, 56–58
  child, 14–16, 38–45, 49–54, 68
  communities, 23–24, 31, 40–41, 54–55
  lineage, 58
  man, 15–16, 38–39, 42–43, 46–48, 61
  Queens, 19, 45–48, 61–62
Black Girl Magic, 67
Black Panther Party (BPP), 18
Black-owned businesses, 31, 35
Blackwall Street, 34
breastfeeding, 44, 49, 52–58, 68
Buckner, Emma, 34
Burrell, Tom, 13

C

Child Support, 38–45, 68
Chinatown, 28
Civic Engagement, 65
Coelho, Paulo, 19
Colfax Massacre (Louisiana), 36
Colostrum, 56–57, 59
controlled opposition, 61

COVID-19, 68
Crow, Jim, 45, 68–69

D

Derogatory, 17, 67
Draft Riot, 36

E

Economic Sovereignty, 22–28, 31, 35, 44, 49, 68
Etymology, 17, 69–70

F

Field Negro, 17–18
First Couple of Days, 56

G

Genetic markers, 54

H

Hasidic Jews, 32
Historically Black College and Universities (H.B.C.U), 1, 5, 63–64
Holy Bible, 69
Holy Koran, 69
hormone oxytocin, 58
House Negro, 17–18
Hurricane Katrina, 68

I

Ignorance, 21

J

Jewish community, 29, 31
Jewish people, 29

K

King of the Zulu Kingdom, 62
King Tut, 62
Kingdom of Madagascar, 62

L

Lincoln, Abraham, 16
Linnaeus, Carl, 70
Little Havana, 28
Little Italy, 28
Lynch, Willie, 15

M

Madhubuti, Haki R, 60
Makeda, 62
Mansa Musa, 62
Melanin, 67
Mexican, 33

N

National Black Economic Development Conference, 36
Nefertiti, 62
New Black Mothers X Blinders, 54

O

Observance, 64
Ocoee Massacre, 36
Oklahoma, 33–34, 67

P

Pennsylvania Child Support Enforcement Program, 40
predominately white institution (P.W.I), 64

Q

Queen of Ancient Egypt, 62
Queen of Sheba, 62

R

Rabbit Hole Deep, 66
racism, 15, 33, 44, 64, 70
Ranavalonna I, 62
Rosewood Massacre, 36

S

Scott, Walter Lamar, 38
Segregation, 33–34
Servitude, 60, 64, 68
Shaka Zulu, 62
So-Called Black Community, 24, 27, 34, 40–41, 49, 55
socio-economics, 28

T

The Clinton Riot of 1875, 36
The Golden Hour, 56
transitional milk, 59
Tulsa, 33–34, 67

W

Weeping Time, 15
West African Mali Empire, 62
Wet Nurses, 52
Williams, John Wesley, 34
Williams, Loula Cotton, 34
Wilmington University, 1

Notes

Notes

Notes

Notes

Notes

Notes

Notes